MANGA *Sparkle*

CREEPY CUTE

ILLUSTRATED BY
K. CAMERO

CASTLE POINT BOOKS
NEW YORK

www.castlepointbooks.com

The Castle Point Books trademark is owned by Castle Point Publishing, LLC.
Castle Point books are published and distributed by St. Martin's Publishing Group.

Special thanks to Kimma Parish.
Design by Katie Jennings Campbell

ISBN 978-1-250-33501-2 (trade paperback)

Our books may be purchased in bulk for promotional, educational, or business use.
Please contact your local bookseller or the Macmillan Corporate and
Premium Sales Department at 1-800-221-7945, extension 5442,
or by email at MacmillanSpecialMarkets@macmillan.com.
First Edition: 2024

10 9 8 7 6 5 4 3 2 1